GROW YOUR OWN *for kids*

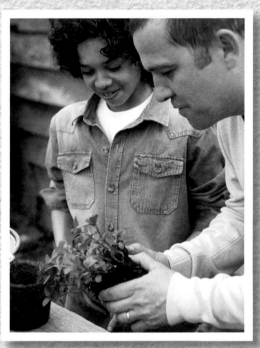

GROW YOUR OWN
for kids

Chris Collins
and Lia Leendertz

Mitchell Beazley

First published in Great Britain in 2012 by
MItchell Beazley, a division of Octopus Publishing Group Ltd
Endeavour House, 189 Shaftesbury Avenue
London WC2H 8JY
www.octopusbooksusa.com

An Hachette UK Company
www.hachette.co.uk

Distributed in the United States by Hachette Book Group USA,
237 Park Avenue, New York, NY 10017, USA

Distributed in Canada by Canadian Media Group,
165 Dufferin Street, Toronto, Ontario, Canada M6K 3H6

ISBN 978-1-84533-606-6

A CIP catalogue record for this book is available from the
British Library

Printed and bound in China

1 3 5 7 9 10 8 6 4 2

Disclaimer
The publishers cannot accept any legal responsibility
or liability for accidents or damage arising from the use
of any items mentioned in this book or in the carrying out
of any of the projects. Some of the projects and recipes
in this book may involve nuts and seeds. Anyone with
a known nut allergy must avoid these. Children under
the age of 3 with a family history of nut allergy, asthma,
eczema, or any type of allergy are also advised to avoid
eating dishes that contain nuts. Do not give whole nuts
or seeds to any child under the age of 5 because of risk
of choking. Adult supervision of children at all times when
gardening, cooking, or carrying out any activity near water
is advised and tools, garden equipment, and dangerous
garden materials such as fertilizers should not be left
where children can access them easily or use them without
adult guidance.

For the RHS:
Publisher: Rae Spencer-Jones
Consultant editor: Simon Maughan

For Octopus Publishing Group:
Publishers: Lorraine Dickey & Alison Starling
Editorial Director: Tracey Smith
Senior Production Controller: Lucy Carter
Art direction and Design: Tracy Killick
Editorial management: Helen Griffin
Editor: Caroline Taggart, Alex Stetter, Joanna Chisholm
Photography: Will Heap

Here's what's inside

Let's get growing!

On a sunny spring morning, it's hard to wait to get outside and check the seedlings that were planted a few days before. It's so exciting! Whether you plant one special sunflower or a whole plot of vegetables, seeing things grow is one of the real wonders of life.

What if I haven't got a garden?

You don't need masses of space or even a garden to be a great gardener – a window-box can give you fresh herbs for pizzas, pasta, salads and sandwiches. Why not try growing a strawberry fountain or use a hanging basket to grow tomatoes? They are great fun to grow and things you pick from your own plants are going to be fresher and far more tasty than anything you can buy in the shops. There is nothing like it! Remember though, give your plants a little bit of your time every day – don't forget to feed, water and give your plants lots of love.

Be a wildlife warrior

When you dig a piece of ground or turn over the soil to take out weeds and stones, it's great fun to watch how many birds you attract to your plot. Bees, butterflies, and other helpful insects can be encouraged to visit your garden by planting certain flowers. In turn, these insects will help your plants to grow by spreading pollen and seeds and eating pests. If you work with wildlife, it will do a lot of the work for you.

Green gardening is great

Nature is very clever but it also needs your help and you can be a green gardener by saving water as you garden. Try to put as much water back into your soil as your plants take out of it. Making compost is fun and if you don't have room for a compost heap, perhaps you can build one at school. Then lots of you can save things from your plants and your kitchen to put onto your heap. You can even make home-made fertilizer for your plants by keeping worms – this book will show you how!

So now you're a gardener

As you pick your first fruit and vegetables, you will see what fun it is to grow things. Everyone loves to be given great things to eat, but don't forget that you can give away some of your baby plants as well – in that way even more people can have fun gardening. Being a gardener will keep you and your friends busy and well fed and there's no better way to enjoy the great world outdoors.

So, welcome to the wonderful world of gardening!

You can start small – why not sow some seeeds in a box for your window sill?

Gardening with other people is even more fun than gardening on your own!

You're going to
be a great
gardener!

setting up a vegetable garden

If you have a garden, your vegetables will do a lot of the work for you, as their roots will search for food and water in the earth. So the first thing for you to do is to learn about your soil.

Where should your garden be?

You may not be able to decide exactly where your vegetable garden will be, but if you can choose, remember a few things. Most vegetables love the sun so pick the sunniest site you can. Plants don't like wind so try to make sure your garden is sheltered. You will need to give your plants lots of water so try to pick an area near to an outdoor faucet or not too far from your house. And one last thing, the roots of large plants and trees use up lots of the goodness in the soil, so keep your veg garden away from them if you can.

What's your soil like?

Squeeze a handful of soil in your hand. If it feels smooth and squelchy, it is probably clay soil. If it feels crumbly and grainy, it is sandy soil. The best soil is not too squelchy and not too grainy, but don't panic if yours is not! You can make any soil better by adding well-rotted compost or manure. Try and grow things that suit your soil type, for example, lots of herbs like sandy soils, and fruit trees prefer growing in clay.

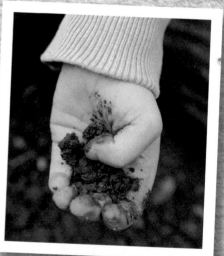

How big is YOUR bed?

Where you plant your vegetables is called a bed. Make sure that yours is small enough for you to reach into the middle without trampling all over the soil. If your bed is bigger than that, you will need to leave a path in the middle. Make sure your path is wide enough to push a wheelbarrow along.

the science

SOIL

Soil is different from one yard to the next, and each soil type is good and bad in different ways. Clay soil is dense, which makes it good at hanging onto nutrients (the food plants need), but it is hard to dig. Sandy soil is very loose, so roots can grow easily, and water drains away quickly. But it loses nutrients quickly and can dry out easily, which means you have to add lots of compost.

Walk along your garden, gently pressing down the soil with your feet

Getting your garden ready

Before you plant anything, you need to make your vegetable garden as perfect as possible. First you need to dig the site to remove weeds and add air, and to help the soil to absorb water. When you have done this, use a rake to get rid of any big stones that have been uncovered by your digging. Finally, walk up and down your bed, pressing the soil back down gently, being careful on tread on every bit of soil.

Gorgeous garden waste

Saving garden waste and turning it into compost to spread over your beds really helps to keep the soil in great condition. But be careful that you use the right ingredients to make it!

Compost is great and, by making it yourself, it is also free!

Piling up the goodness

Great compost needs the right ingredients and plenty of air. If you don't have both of these, it will be slimy and smelly. Use a mixture of things that rot quickly (like grass clippings and even food from your kitchen) and things that will take longer to rot but will help to keep plenty of air in your compost pile (like straw, twigs, or cardboard).

Designing your compost bin

You *can* just throw your compost ingredients into a pile, but a compost bin is neater and works better. Storing compost in a bin helps to build up heat in the pile, which makes it rot down more quickly. Homemade bins made from slatted lumber let air into the pile and are great (make sure it has a door in the front so you can get to your compost), but you can buy plastic ones that work well too.

Cover your pile to heat it up and it will make compost more quickly

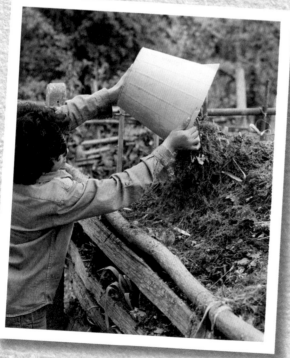

Turning the compost pile

To make compost quickly, you must turn your compost over after a few months. This will help to get air right into the middle of the pile, which keeps the temperature up. To do this, first take away the bin, or the front of it, dig out all the compost, put the bin back, and then put all the compost back in it. Phew.

In the pile or out? Friend or enemy?

IN	OUT
Leaf trimmings	Cooked food
Grass clippings	Fruit
Raw veg peelings	Eggs
Thin twigs and straw	Meat
Newspaper	Thick tree prunings
Cardboard	Plastic

Spreading the goodness

Once you've made your compost and it's ready to use, you need to spread it around the garden where needed. Use a bucket to take it to your beds from the compost pile and then use a fork to mix it into the garden dirt. This will help your soil to stay in tip-top condition—it's a bit like giving it a huge dose of vitamins!

Homemade compost is health food for your garden

13

How high is your bed?

If your soil isn't good enough or you want to have a small garden to call your own, you could make a raised bed and fill it with soil-based potting mix, which you can buy in garden centers.

Working in the garden with your friends is fun

1 BEFORE YOU CAN START TO USE YOUR RAISED BED, cover the base in thick cardboard. This will kill any grass and weeds underneath it. Then fill the bed with potting soil. Rake the soil carefully to get rid of any stones or lumps.

2 NOW TREAD DOWN THE SOIL TO GET RID OF ANY POCKETS OF AIR. It's more fun to do this with your friends. Now try to be patient—it's best to let the contents settle for a week or two. You may then need to top up the potting soil.

To make a raised bed, you need help from an adult who is good at DIY

3 TO HELP YOU TO PLANT IN STRAIGHT LINES use garden twine tied to two sticks. Put one stick at each end of the line you want to mark and push the sticks into the potting soil, pulling the twine tight as you do so.

Building a raised bed

If you don't have a special kit, perhaps an adult will agree to make a raised bed for you. To do this, mark out the sides of the bed, then use a spade to clear away any grass from where the raised bed's walls are going to lie. A level will help to get the area roughly flat. Lay four boards on the ground. Drill holes through the ends and use long, heavy-duty screws to fix the boards together as shown. A corner brace will add strength. Make the beds the depth of a single board, or stack several "frames" on top of one another and secure them together to make something deeper.

4 IT'S EASY TO LOOK AFTER YOUR PLANTS IN A RAISED BED because you won't have to walk on top of your young seedlings and you can just reach into the middle of the bed without bending too far.

15

Tubs, pots, and containers

Don't worry if you don't have a vegetable garden. Lots of plants will grow really well in pots or other containers on balconies or windowsills. Perhaps your school will have room for some too.

Choosing your pot

Always pick a big pot. Small amounts of potting soil dry out quickly, so plants in small pots will need more attention than those in larger ones. But you must be careful not to let the soil in any container dry out.

Letting the water out

Roots will rot if the soil in a container is too damp. Check that your pots have a hole in the bottom to let water out. (If they don't, ask an adult to make some for you.) Put broken pieces of old pots over the holes to stop the water from washing away the soil.

What to plant in?

Any good-quality, soil-based potting mix is ideal, and it is available at any garden center or even in some large supermarkets.

Use your fingers to break up any big lumps in your soil

Use bits of broken plant pots—or even small stones—to help water to drain away from your pots

16

the science

PLANTING IN POTS

Plants growing in pots (rather than in the ground) need a bit more attention and care. Make sure the soil is firm when you do your planting and press out all of the air pockets. This allows water to travel through the soil easily and be taken up by the plants' roots. Always leave a gap at the top of the pot for watering—if you don't, the water will overflow and wash the soil from the pot.

Plants to eat that grow well in pots

Blueberries

Carrots

Chili peppers

Citrus trees

Dwarf bush beans

Eggplants

Herbs

Lettuce

Scallions

Strawberries

Sweet peppers

Tomatoes

Zucchini

Hanging baskets

These are great for plants such as tomatoes and strawberries that naturally "trail" and hang. They will dry out quickly, though, as there isn't a lot of space for much soil in them, so you will need to water them even more than plants in pots.

Unusual and "free" pots

Keep your eyes open around your home for other things you can use as containers for plants. Old crates, unused sinks, large tins, and old colanders all make great containers. You could even try using some old rubber boots!

Great plants for tiny spaces

Don't worry if you don't have a garden of your own. There are lots of plants that will grow happily in pots or other containers on a patio, balcony, or even a windowsill.

make the most of the space you have on your windowsill

Picking your pot

Always choose the biggest possible pot. Small amounts of potting soil dry out quickly, so plants in small pots need a lot more attention than those in larger ones. Above all, you have to be careful not to let the soil in any container dry out completely.

Pots as decorations

Try to choose different sorts of containers for indoor windowsills as they will be on show and it's good if they are prettier—and cleaner—than outdoor flowerpots!

Choosing the potting soil

Try to match the potting soil to the crops you want to grow. Most vegetables are happy with any good-quality potting mix, but acid-loving fruits such as blueberries prefer an acidic-soil mix. Longer-term crops such as apples and pears will need a soil-based potting mix, and you can replace the top layer of soil each year to refresh the nutrients. Soilless mixes are kinder to the environment.

You can put your containers in a place where it is easy to reach your crops and pick them to eat

Hanging baskets

These are great for growing cherry tomatoes, especially if you don't have much room. Hanging baskets will also keep your plants safe from slugs and snails, who like to nibble their leaves. Just make sure that the basket is not in the way—you don't want someone to hit their head—and remember to water your plants regularly.

Containers that used to be something else*

Rubber boots
Old shoes
Wheelbarrows
Trash can lids
Tin bathtubs
Clean tin cans
Wooden crates

Kitchen colanders
Automobile tires

*But make sure that no one else wants to use them before you start planting!

19

Get growing!

Get yourself kitted out

You can get started with just a few things. The tools sold for adults to use can be very heavy so, if you can, it's a great idea to get your own set in a size that's just right for you. Why not ask for a brightly colored hand fork and trowel for your next birthday?

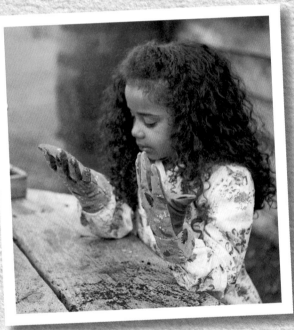

Peasticks These are twiggy branches that are used to support plants such as peas.

Labels It's very easy to forget what you have planted. Write a label—old popsicle sticks are perfect for this—and mark where you have put things as soon as you can.

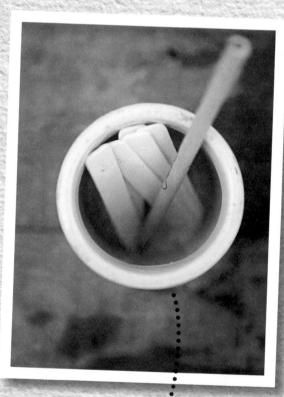

Gloves Even if you love getting your hands dirty, you will need gloves for some jobs in the garden to stop your hands from getting scratched or stung by nettles.

Dibble A dibble is a piece of wood that is used to make small holes in the soil to drop in seeds or small plants into. A popsicle stick, a pencil, or even a plant stem can be used to do the same job.

keep a stock of labels so you can mark your planting as soon as it is done

Watering can Seedlings and plants moved to new holes need watering. For seedlings, use a water breaker nozzle (added to the hose or watering can). This lets the water out in lots of tiny streams, which won't damage the seedlings). Take off the water breaker to puddle water around larger plants.

23

Spades Spades are used to dig holes, to dig up plants, to turn over the soil, or to break it up. You can also use a spade to move compost around the yard.

Fork Forks are used for digging too, but they are more useful than spades for weedy ground, especially where there are lots of perennial weed roots that shouldn't be chopped up.

Hand trowel This is a mini spade that can be held easily in one hand. You can use a trowel to make small holes for small plants.

Hand fork A hand fork is a mini version of a full-sized fork. It fits easily in your hand and is used for digging around older plants.nts.

Rake A rake is the perfect tool for making sure your bed is free of stones.

Try to find a spade that is smaller than an adult-sized one. You can even get ones that have handles that you can make longer as you grow taller

Your rake is especially useful in a new bed to make sure there are no stones or clumps of compost in the soil

Your hand trowel is your best friend. You can use it for all sorts of jobs in the yard

You can manage without a hoe but they are extremely handy and can be used for all sorts of jobs, from weeding to helping you move soil when you are planting

A hand fork is the same size as a hand trowel and just as useful, especially for levering out stubborn roots from pots

mister You can only water really tiny seedlings with a very fine spray like the one from a mister. Otherwise, the little plants will be washed away.

seed flats Use these for sowing seeds. Fill a seed flat with potting mix and then sow your seeds onto the surface.

Pots You can sow big seeds such as sunflowers straight into pots.

Riddle Use a garden riddle to get rid of lumps from potting mix when you are planting seeds.

Twine You use garden twine to mark out lines to sow along and to support some kinds of climbing plants; also, to tie canes together to make a tepee to support plants like beans.

25

Start seeds indoors while it's cold outside

While the soil is cold in spring you can start seeds in containers indoors. You can plant them in the ground outside when the weather warms up.

Seed flat or pot?

Small seeds need to be sown in seed flats and moved to pots when they have grown into small plants. Big seeds, like these bean seeds, should be planted straight into pots early in spring. They don't like cold soil so you have to keep them safe until the soil is warm enough to move the small plants into your veg garden. Fill the pots with seed starter mix: It is finer than all-purpose potting mix and contains fewer nutrients, so the roots will grow large searching for food.

Gently fill the pots with fine seed starter mix

Reading the packet

Every seed needs different things. Some should be sown on the surface of the potting mix, some covered with a fine dusting of mix, while others should be pushed below the surface. Always read the packet carefully!

Sowing from the palm

When you are sowing seeds, tip them out of the packet and onto your hand before sowing. If they are big, you should put only one or two on the surface of the potting mix in each pot. Try to put them into the middle, so that the seeds have the same amount of room around each one. Then push each seed around ¾in. into the soil and gently cover the hole with a little potting mix.

Watering after sowing

Once you have sown your seeds, they need water. A flood of water would churn up the soil, so use a fine water breaker, which will turn the gush of water into a sprinkle. Another way to water flats is to run a couple of inches of water into a sink and leave the flat soaking for half an hour. After watering them, put the containers on a light windowsill or in a sunroom or greenhouse until they sprout (germinate).

Label the seeds and let them germinate on a well-lit windowsill

27

Sowing your seeds outside

From seeds to vegetables in one spot

Sowing seeds straight into the ground is much simpler than sowing them indoors. Lots of seeds are strong enough to sow outdoors (like lots of lettuces, carrots, and beans) but some are not. Always check your seed packet before you plant.

Before you begin

Before you sow anything, make sure there are no weeds in your garden as they will fight your seedlings for light and water. Give your plants the best chance by providing them with a weed-free home where they can live without fighting for space.

Preparing the bed

Sowing your seeds in a straight line helps you to spot any weeds that invade the bed. Tie a piece of twine to two sticks and then stretch it across your bed, pushing the sticks into the ground at each end. Following the line, use a trowel or a spade to make a long hole or trench in the soil (known as a "drill") into which you can sow your seeds.

Use twine tied on two sticks and pull it tight to mark a straight line

Sowing your seeds

Pour some seeds into your hand and pick a few up with the fingertips of your other hand. Sprinkle the seeds as evenly as you can along the drill, following the instructions on the packet for how many to sprinkle.

Settling in your seeds

Cover your seeds with a little soil, then water along the line using a water breaker for a gentle rain of water. Write a label immediately as it is very easy to forget what you have planted.

Thinning the baby plants out

However thinly you sow your seeds, you will almost always need to take some of the weaker-looking plants out later to make more room for the others. To do this, carefully take some of the seedlings out of your row so that the ones left have the same space on each side of them, and that space looks the same as the seed packet tells you it should be. Do this when the seedlings are small and water them straight afterwards.

It may seem cruel, but you need to take out some baby plants to let the others grow

the science

THINNING OUT

Some seedlings such as carrots and lettuce benefit from a little competition after germination. When sowing, we use more seed than we need, and once the plants start to grow we thin out and remove the weaker seedlings, leaving only the strongest. This gives individual plants the space they require to produce big, healthy crops. Not all the thinnings go to waste—little bits of lettuce can go into a sandwich, but carrot seedlings should be put on the compost pile.

Looking after baby plants

As soon as seeds you have sown indoors have germinated (started to sprout), you will need to look after them carefully so that they produce strong leaves and roots and will be able to fend for themselves in the outside world.

Moving home

Moving a seedling from the crowded seed flat into its own pot is called "pricking on." You should do this as soon as the first leaves appear on the tiny plant. Hold the seedling by the leaf (never by the stem as it can easily be damaged). Gently push a dibble into the dirt under the seedling and use it to help move the plant out of the potting mix from its roots. A popsicle stick or a pencil will also work if you don't have a dibble.

seedlings need to be looked after carefully, especially when they are very young

the science

BABY PLANTS
Some young plants like cucumbers and tomatoes need extra protection from the cold. This is why their seeds are often sown indoors. We describe these plants as "tender." Others are stronger and don't mind colder temperatures—we call them "hardy." Hardy plants like radishes or lettuces can be sown straight into the ground. Remember to read the seed packet to find out if your plants will be tender or hardy.

Preparing a new home for your plant

Fill a small pot with potting mix and tap it gently on the table top. This will help the mix to settle. Use your dibble to make a hole big enough to hold your seedling's roots in the potting mix, and then gently put the plant into the hole. We've used homemade newspaper pots for our young seedlings and you can find out exactly how to make these on pages 76–7.

If you don't have a dibble, use a plant stem, a twig, or even a pencil

settling in

Use your fingertips to firm the potting mix gently around the seedling, taking care around its delicate stem. Add a label to the pot straight away and then water your baby plant using a fine water breaker. If you don't have one, ask an adult to make lots of little holes in the lid of a jar so that you can use this to sprinkle water on your plant.

It's tough out there ...

Plants can get a bit of a shock when they are moved outdoors as it's much colder. Getting your plants ready to be planted outside is called "hardening off." in late spring, when the weather is a bit warmer, put them outside for an hour or so on a warm day, then move them in when the sun goes down. Gradually increase the time your plants spend outside, always moving them back inside at night. After a week or so you can leave them out in a sheltered spot overnight for a few nights and, after this, they should be ready to live outside full time.

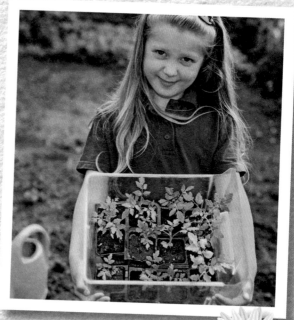

31

Watering wisely

Watering plants at the right time and in the right way stops waste and helps your plants to grow. Why not collect and use rainwater? Your plants will love it and you will be helping the planet too.

When to water

Always try to water your plants in the morning or evening as in the middle of the day, when it is hot and sunny, lots of the water you add will evaporate before the plants' roots have time to absorb it. Some vegetable plants such as zucchini and lettuces can turn moldy if you leave water sitting on their leaves overnight. Make sure you water these in the morning, so that the leaves are completely dry by evening. Basil is the one plant that should be watered in the middle of the day but never in the evening—it hates going to bed with wet feet.

Where to water

A clever way to be sure that plants in pots are getting only the water they need is to put them on a saucer and pour water into that, instead of onto the surface of the soil. The roots then absorb the water they need, leaving behind any they don't. An hour or so after you have added water, check the saucer and pour out any that is left over.

It's a good idea to add water to a saucer under your plants as then they will only use what they need

It is better to add a lot of water once a week to your veg garden than to add little dribbles of water every day

Saving water

You can buy special rain barrels to put in your yard to collect rainwater. Water is so precious that we should try to save as much as we can. If you don't have a rain barrel, remember that you can also recycle clean waste water from the kitchen on your plants—but remember that they won't like soapy or greasy water!

When have you watered enough?

When you are growing plants in pots, you need to know how much water they require so that you don't give them too little or too much. Remember that even if the soil on the surface of the pot is dry, there may still be plenty of moisture lower down. Poke your finger into the potting mix and if it feels damp you don't need to add more water. If it feels dry, you do.

How to weed and feed to grow superplants

Just like us, plants need plenty of food to help them to grow. Gardeners call these foods nutrients. You can find nutrients in soil, but they get used up easily, so we put them back by adding fertilizers. Plants also have to fight weeds for nutrients, water, and light ... so remove weeds!

Two great ways to get rid of weeds

A hoe is a tool that is useful for clearing big patches of weeds. It slices off the tops of the weeds. Weed in between plants using a hand fork (a small fork that, as its name implies, sits in your hand), as you can be more careful not to cause any damage to the plants you want to keep. It's best to weed on a hot day as the sun will dry out any weeds you pull out and stop them from growing again.

Make sure that you dig out the whole root

the science

ORGANIC FERTILIZERS

There are lots of different fertilizers that all do different jobs. Liquid fertilizers are mixed with water. Some, like seaweed extract, are sprayed onto the leaves—they contain magnesium and iron, which are needed to make chlorophyll, a green pigment that helps plants to create nutrients. You can also add bone meal or soybean meal directly to your soil—these will supply nutrients like nitrogen, which is important for leaves, and phosphorus, which is vital for roots.

Target the flowers

Some weeds spread using underground stems that you need to dig out, but many spread through their seeds. If you see a weed with flowers on, it is about to produce seeds that will grow into more weeds. So it makes sense to get rid of the weeds with flowers first.

Liquid goodness

Plants can be given a boost of nutrients, which can be added to your watering can. Mix it up, pour it on your plants, and it will be taken in through their roots. Do this every few weeks in the growing season. Solid fertilizers work more slowly, but they feed plants over a long time. This sort of fertilizer is often included in potting mixes, but you can also buy plugs of them to push into the soil.

You need to measure liquid fertilizer carefully. Don't be afraid to ask for help

Use a mister to spray the leaves with liquid fertilizer every two weeks

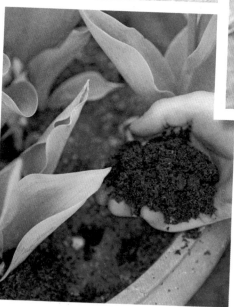

An extra boost for your pots

The soil in containers can get very low in nutrients. Potted plants need feeding every week, but you should also add a "dressing" of a few handfuls of fresh potting mix to the top of your pots every spring. This is called topdressing.

Tasty, fresh food you have grown yourself

The best thing about growing your own food is eating it, especially if you started by planting seeds. Fruit and vegetables taste better when you have picked them yourself—they will be fresher than anything you can find in the supermarkets and will have far more flavor.

Pick them only when they are ripe

When you buy fruit and vegetables from a supermarket, they may have been picked quite a long time before they were ripe. This is done so that crops can be carried to the stores without being damaged and so that they will keep well, giving supermarkets the longest possible time to sell them. But because they haven't ripened in the ground or on the plant, they are not likely to be nearly as tasty as when you can eat them just after you have picked them yourself. When you grow your own crops, you don't have to worry about how long it will take to get them to your kitchen and you can leave them to grow until they are absolutely at their best.

Harvesting from under the ground

Vegetables like beet and carrots (called root crops because you are actually eating their roots) can be picked when they are small and tender in summer or left in the ground until winter. You can pick them from the same row at any time; you don't have to dig them all at once. In summer, use a hand fork to help pull up the carrots you would like to eat. This will also make the plants less crowded, giving the ones that remain more room to grow. Eat the carrots you take out and leave the rest until the fall or winter.

Harvesting leafy greens

Leafy greens should be eaten as fresh as possible. Pick them carefully and your homegrown leaves will stay fresh until you are ready to eat them later the same day (try not to keep them overnight as they will go floppy and won't be nearly as good). Looseleaf lettuce can be picked by cutting at the base of each leaf with scissors. These leaves, which will regrow, are also known as cut-and-come-again leaves as you can go back to the same plant for more, time and time again.

Eat things immediately

Many vegetables start to become less tasty from the moment that you pick them, either because they start to lose their natural sugars or because they get tougher. Except for pears, which ripen off the tree, fruit should also be eaten as soon as possible after picking it because it can become mushy if you leave it even for a few days.

Tasty, fresh peas— sweet and delicious!

Brilliant plants that will get you growing

Here are some of the simplest and tastiest fruits, vegetables, and herbs you can grow. If you don't know where to start, these pages will give you some ideas. And don't forget, you can always try growing other things once you've got the hang of growing these.

Snow peas

These crunchy green pods are eaten whole when they are young and sweet. They are great to grow as a vegetable-garden snack.

Winter squash and pumpkin

These fruits grow large over the summer and are picked in the fall and winter to eat or carve for Halloween. When they are roasted, they taste sweet and nutty.

Potatoes

Homegrown potatoes taste so much better than any you can buy and it is really exciting finding the "buried treasure" of waxy early potatoes under the ground.

Garlic

Pizzas and pasta sauces are twice as tasty when made with homegrown garlic.

Snow peas are tasty eaten straight from the plant

Garlic is very easy to grow

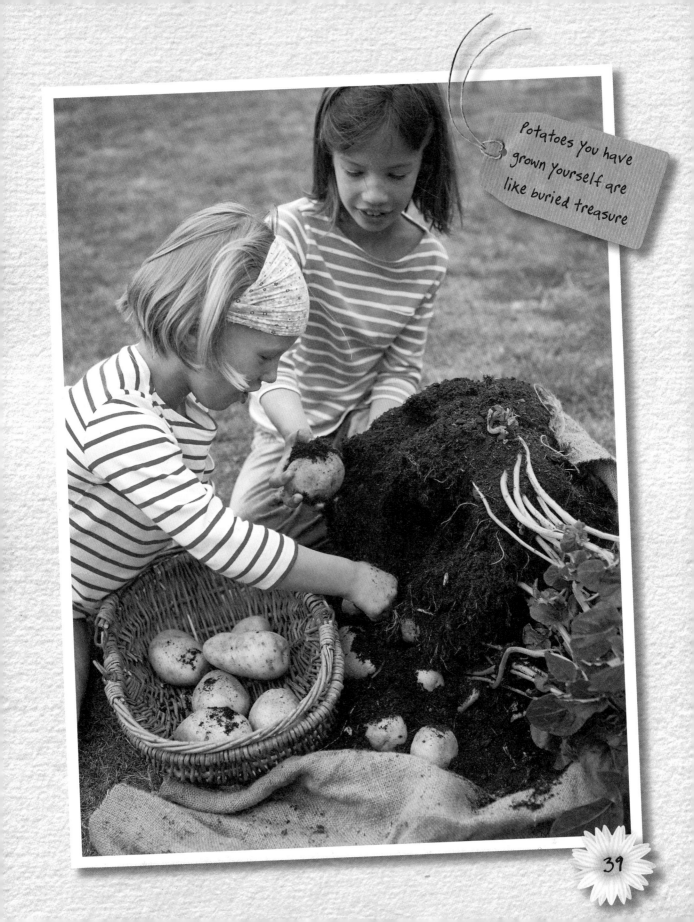

Potatoes you have grown yourself are like buried treasure

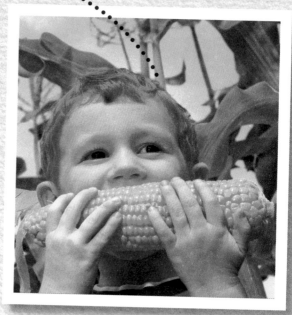

Corn is great fun to grow AND to eat, too

perfectly ripe cherry tomatoes

Cherry tomatoes

One of the stars of your vegetable and fruit garden! Nothing tastes quite as good as a fresh, ripe, homegrown tomato.

Cucumbers

Grow cucumbers that have small fruit, either in a greenhouse or outdoors, and you can enjoy sweet, crunchy cucumber all summer.

Carrots

Carrots are best picked and eaten in summer, when they are young. They grow well in deep pots if you don't have a vegetable garden.

Fava beans

Pick these when they are young and tender. Taking the beans out of their pods is fun too—the insides of their pods are furry.

Corn

Corn is really tasty when it is cooked and eaten just after it has been picked. It is delicious when you cook it on the barbecue.

Leafy greens

You can grow and eat different leafy greens almost year-round. They vary in flavor from mild lettuce to spicy oriental leaves.

Basil

Grow lots of basil and add handfuls of it to pasta or to put on top of pizzas. It is also tasty when added to salads with tomatoes.

Rosemary

Rosemary looks like a tough and woody herb but it has bags of flavor when you add it to food while it is cooking sunflowers grow quickly and will probably be the tallest flowers in your garden

Why not make your own strawberry cream tea?

Mint

If you like the taste of toothpaste or chewing gum, you will love mint. You can eat it fresh in salads, on potatoes, or on top of berries!

Thyme

Thyme is used a lot in Italian food—pizzas and pasta wouldn't be the same without it.

Blueberries

Blueberries taste just as sweet and delicious straight off the bush as they do in muffins or cakes. The only bad thing is that they will only be ready to eat for two weeks every summer.

Strawberries

Try to let strawberries turn a glorious glossy red before popping them in your mouth. But it's hard to keep your hands off them.

Raspberries

Raspberries are easy to grow and will give you huge numbers of delicious summer and fall fruits—gorgeous with ice cream.

Edible flowers

There are lots of flowers that can be eaten and others that definitely cannot. Check with a grown-up before eating any flowers, but marigolds, violas, nasturtiums, and chive flowers can all be eaten and look lovely in salads or to decorate your plate.

Sunflowers

As well as for their huge, bright flowers, you should grow sunflowers for their seeds, which are really tasty after they have been roasted. And why not have a competition with a friend to find out whose sunflower grows the tallest or the fastest?

Projects to
grow Your own

A window box full of herbs

A sunny window box is the perfect spot for growing herbs. But be careful that it is secured safely to the windowsill as you don't want it to fall off and hit someone passing by!

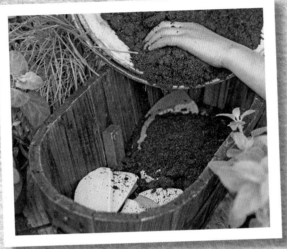

the science

ADDING GRIT FOR DRAINAGE

You can learn a lot about plants by doing some homework on where they come from. Thyme, rosemary, and a number of other herbs come from hot dry places like the Mediterranean, where the soil is very stony and water drains quickly. That is why these plants don't like having wet feet. Adding gravel to the potting mix you use will help it to drain more quickly and make a home from home for your herbs. You can also buy ready-mixed gritty potting mix from the garden center.

1 PUT BITS OF BROKEN TERRA-COTTA POTS OR SMALL STONES over the drainage holes in the base of your window box. These will add drainage and stop the soil washing out. Half fill the box with potting mix mixed with several handfuls of grit. Press it down lightly all over.

2 PUSH THE PLANTS OUT OF THEIR CONTAINERS FROM THE BASE and put them in the window box, trying out different arrangements until you like the way it looks. Trailing plants look good at either end, and more upright plants are best in the center. Mint and basil should be planted in their own pots—mint grows strongly and may use too much space, while basil needs careful watering and it will be happiest growing on its own.

Keep your window box in a sunny spot to give it the best light

3 ONCE YOU HAVE ARRANGED YOUR HERBS, use the same gritty potting mix to carefully fill in around the plants, firming down the soil with your fingers as you go. When you have finished, the soil should be a few inches below the top of the window box.

4 WATER YOUR PLANTS WELL and put the window box safely on a wide windowsill or support it with brackets. Make certain that it cannot fall off and hit anyone beneath the window. Make sure that you keep your window box watered.

Yum!

Tasty pasta sauce   Add some basil leaves to the top of your tomato pasta sauce

Sour cream and chive dip   Snip chives into sour cream for a quick and tasty snack.

5 THE WONDERFUL THING ABOUT HERBS is that they love to be harvested. If you snip or pinch off the newest, freshest leaves or sprigs the plants grow even bushier. So harvest them regularly. Chives grow differently from other herbs, more like grass, and you should snip the leaves from the base with a pair of scissors.

Nonstop leafy greens

Cut-and-come-again leafy greens are those that can be harvested several times from one sowing. You just cut what you need and the remaining plant grows back. Leafy greens grow quickly and are always fresher and tastier than anything you can buy at the supermarket. Why not try writing your name or initials in tasty little seedlings?

You can use a garden riddle to make sure your potting mix is free of stones and clumps of soil

1 FILL A WINDOW BOX almost to the top with soil-based potting mix. If you want to, you can use sand to mark out your name, initials, or a pattern in the top of the potting mix where you are going to sow your seeds.

2 POUR SOME SEEDS INTO YOUR HAND and pinch small amounts of them between the fingers of your other hand. Scatter them along the marked-out lines of sand, cover them lightly with potting mix, then water.

3 WHEN THE SEEDS GERMINATE, thin the tiny plants out a little, taking a few away so that each plant is about 2in. from its neighbor. Eat these "thinnings" as baby leafy greens.

Cut your leafy greens regularly and they will grow straight back

4 TO HARVEST, use a pair of scissors to cut only what you want to eat in your next meal, popping it instantly into a plastic bag. Now wash your leaves. Fill the sink with cold water and add some ice cubes. Tip the leaves into the water and leave them for 10–20 minutes. They will fill with water and be crunchy.

If you choose the right plants, you can harvest leafy greens almost year-round. In winter the leaves become tough, but they will be better quality and more tempting if you can grow them under cover. You can buy mini hoop houses and temporary row covers if you don't have a greenhouse.

Spring—pea shoots, baby spinach
Summer—basil and lots of varieties of lettuce
Fall and winter (in a greenhouse, or under protective covers)—oriental leaves, hardy lettuce

Tasty salads from seeds

You don't even need a windowsill to grow good things to eat—you can sprout seeds indoors and pick them at your table. Try growing some as "micro leaves" that you can pick as tiny plants and eat others as just-sprouted seeds.

You will need a seed flat and some paper towel

Growing cress and micro leaves

Sprouting seeds that you want to turn into green plants need plenty of light. Soak the seeds in water overnight, then scatter them thinly on damp paper towel in a shallow seed flat. You don't need potting mix. Put the flat on an inside windowsill and once your plants have rooted make sure to keep the paper towel moist.

Before you sow some types of seeds you will need to soak them in water overnight

scatter your seeds evenly by tapping the side of your hand

Not enough light?

You can grow sprouting seeds in glass jars or burlap bags as they don't need light. Soak the seeds in water overnight, then rinse and drain them. Put them in your jar or bag and rinse and drain them with fresh water every morning and evening for between three to eight days, depending on the variety. The seeds will swell up, so don't use too many. You can eat the sprouted seeds right away.

Time to pick

Some seed sprouts will be ready to pick after three days and others may need as long as ten. Pick the ones first that have grown the most and leave the others to grow a bit more. In this way you will get a few meals out of each batch. Rinse the seed sprouts well and eat them immediately, or store them in a plastic bag in the refrigerator for up to a week, rinsing them in clean water every few days.

Tiny micro leaves and sprouted seeds to try

Seeds that you can sprout in a jar: chickpeas, barley, lentils, mung beans
Micro leaves that you can sprout on a seed flat: cress, wheatgrass, radish, alfalfa, buckwheat

How can I eat them?

Use sprouted seeds raw, either to add extra flavor to salad, or you can add them as a topping to a stir-fry.

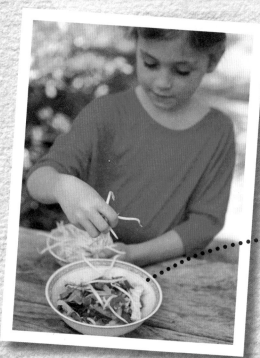

sprouted seeds like beansprouts are deliciously crunchy

49

Growing perfect potatoes

Potatoes grow really well in a sack or another large container. Your potatoes will grow faster than they do in the ground and won't be attacked by slugs, so you will get the best possible result.

start "presprouting" your potatoes in early spring

1 BUY SPECIAL "SEED" POTATOES from the garden center. To give them the best start you can presprout them before planting. To do this, put your potatoes in egg cartons or on a seed flat and leave them in a cool, light, frost-free place for a few weeks.

2 IN MIDSPRING YOU CAN PLANT YOUR POTATOES OUT. Fill the base of your container with about 8in. of potting mix (you can reuse old mix for this, if you want).

When to eat them

Potatoes taste quite different depending on whether they are picked early or late in the year. For new potatoes with soft skins that will need to be eaten immediately, harvest your potatoes after flowering has stopped. For larger potatoes with tougher skins wait until the leaves have yellowed and died down before picking. These are great to store.

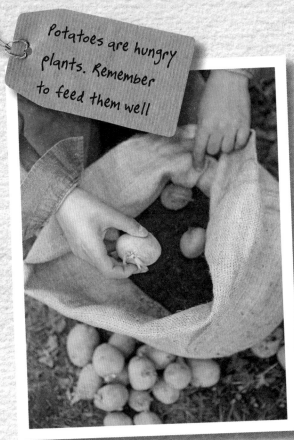

3 PUT THREE SEED POTATOES ON TOP of the potting mix, evenly spaced, and cover them with another 4in. of mix. Water them well after you have planted them.

4 AS THEIR STEMS GROW UNDERGROUND, potatoes will grow along them. If they are exposed to the light they will turn green and become poisonous, so you need to keep covering them up with more potting mix. Do this at least once a week. Water them often and add a liquid feed once or twice a week.

Cover the stems with more soil as they grow

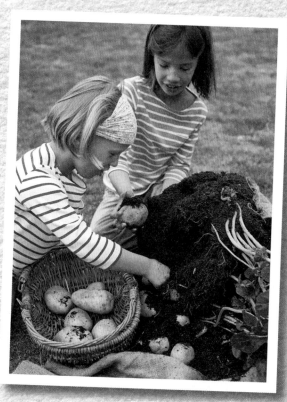

5 TO PICK YOUR POTATOES, tip the soil out of the container and dig around with your hands to find the potatoes. If you ask an adult to start boiling some water before you harvest your potatoes, you can eat them in as little as 15 minutes after they come out of the soil!

51

Grow tiny sweet tomatoes in a hanging basket

"Sungold" tomatoes grow perfectly in a hanging basket, their stems trailing down, covered with cherry-sized fruits. It's a brilliant way to grow tomatoes in a small space, but you have to be careful to water them.

You need one plant and suitable potting mix per basket

Plant some small flowers with your tomatoes to make your baskets colorful

1 LINE A HANGING BASKET, making sure there are holes in the base of your liner, and put a small circle of tough plastic cut from a grocery sack over them. If the basket liner has no holes, ask an adult to use a screwdriver to make some to let water drain away.

2 FILL THE HANGING BASKET WITH SOIL-BASED POTTING MIX. Run the potting mix through your fingers to make sure that there are no big lumps in the soil.

52

3 MAKE A HOLE IN THE POTTING MIX and plant the young tomato plant in it, pressing gently on the soil with your hands to make it firm. If you have more than one basket to fill, just use one plant in each. Why not plant flowers at the same time?

Plant lots of hanging baskets and you will have tomatoes all summer long

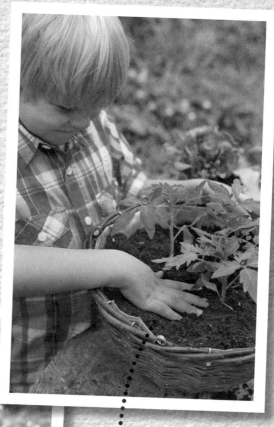

Press the potting mix down gently around your plants

4 TOMATOES NEED PLENTY OF FOOD AND WATER so water your baskets every day. When the flowers start to turn into fruits, feed with liquid 5–5–10, which is high in potassium, or with liquid comfrey. Feed your tomatoes every week from now on.

Always water your baskets with a gentle sweep as the rush of water might be too much for your plants to cope with

53

5 IF YOU CHOOSE SPECIAL HANGING-BASKET TOMATOES YOU WON'T NEED TO DO THIS, but if you grow other types of tomatoes in the ground, in pots, or in compost bags, "pinch off" the topshoots as they grow (this means that you should pull away the tiny new shoots) as this will make the plant bushy rather than too tall and will help fruit to grow.

special "trailing" tomatoes grow well in a hanging basket but there's not much soil so you need to water them every day

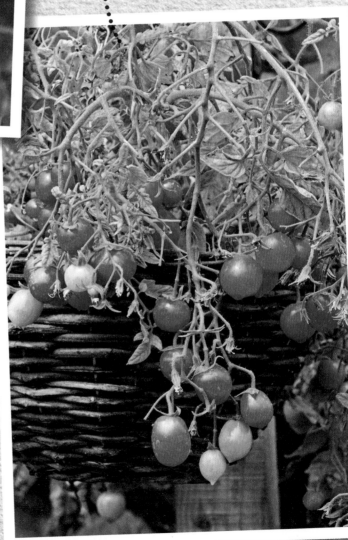

the science

PINCHING OFF SIDESHOOTS

You can stop your tomato plants from wasting energy growing too many stems by pulling off ("pinching off") little sideshoots, like in this picture. Flowers and then tomatoes will grow only on the stems that are left. By doing this, your plant will send all the nutrients it has absorbed to a smaller number of tomatoes, and they will grow bigger, stronger, and even more tasty.

Yum!

Homemade tomato sauce   Chop an onion into tiny pieces and fry it gently in some olive oil. Add your tomatoes and bash them with a spoon to break them up. Add black pepper and some chili flakes and, after 20 minutes, take the sauce from the heat. When it is cool, whizz it in a blender so that your sauce has no lumps. Although it's tasty cold, like homemade catsup, you can also heat your sauce up and eat it with pasta and grated cheese. Yummy!

Tomato tart   Put a frozen puff-paste sheet on a cookie sheet, prick it all over with a fork, spread it with some tomato purée or your homemade tomato sauce. Put slices of your tomatoes all over the top and then add some of your homegrown herbs and some grated cheese. You could also add mushrooms or other vegetables. After 20 minutes in a medium-hot oven, your tart should be ready to eat!

6 SMALL CHERRY TOMATOES ARE THE FIRST TO RIPEN. They will become sweeter the longer they are left to grow, so don't be too eager to eat them. Pick them only when they are perfectly red, and pop them into your mouth or into a salad.

Growing crunchy cucumbers

Cucumbers grow upwards *and* sideways. Make sure you choose a type that likes to be planted outdoors and give it plenty of room.

You will need a really big pot or ideally space in a raised bed, canes or old broom handles, twine, cucumber plants

save old broom handles and use these instead of canes

1 CUCUMBERS NEED lots of room. In late spring, find a sunny spot for your young plants in a raised bed or the biggest pot you can use. (Remember, if you have grown your young plants from seed, make sure they are big and strong enough before you think about planting them outside.)

2 USE CANES OR OLD BROOM HANDLES TO MAKE A SUPPORT for your plants to climb. Fill a large pot with potting mix and push three canes into it. (You can also do this in the ground.) Tie the canes with twine at the top and then twice more further down, looping the twine around the canes to create a kind of rope ladder. Plant one plant at the foot of each cane.

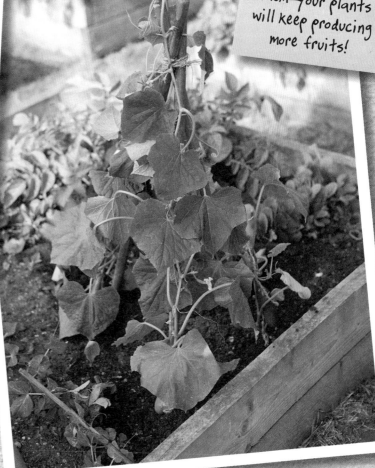

Plant cucumbers out in early summer then keep picking them—your plants will keep producing more fruits!

3 CUCUMBERS CONTAIN MASSES OF WATER—that's why they're so juicy. Give them lots of water every day when it's hot. They also like plenty of nutrients, so feed them once a week with liquid 5–5–10 or liquid comfrey.

Pick your cucumbers when they are small and sweet—perfect for a snack!

4 TIE THE CUCUMBER STEMS into your cane-and-twine "tepee" as they grow. Loop the twine around the stem and then make another loop around the support—this will look like a figure eight. The twine "eight" stops the cucumber from rubbing against the hard cane. Carefully harvest the fruits when they are still small, using scissors or pruners.

Beans may need support!

Most beans climb high and need tall, strong supports. These are simple to make but can be a bit fiddly, so why not ask an adult to help you? It is best to sow your bean seeds indoors in pots to give them the greatest chance of success.

1 FIRST YOU NEED TO MAKE A SUPPORT FOR YOUR BEANS. Make a long "tent" from bamboo canes, tying them where they cross over at the top and adding a flat pole to the top as the picture on the opposite page shows. If you are sowing seeds directly in the ground, you should plant two seeds at the bottom of each cane and cover them with temporary row cover, as they are tender and need to be kept warm. If you have grown your seeds in pots, put one plant at the bottom of each cane.

the science

"FOLLOW-ON" SOWING
If you sow a long row of seeds all at the same time, they will all mature at the same time too. Nobody wants to eat beans every day, but if you leave them on the plant they turn tough and stringy. "Follow-on" sowing is a way of staggering harvesting time so you get a small amount of perfect beans. It works only with plants such as snap beans that crop quite quickly. Make a small early sowing under row cover in midspring, and repeat every few weeks until mid- to late summer.

2 IT IS BETTER TO SOW YOUR BEAN SEEDS INDOORS IN POTS. Then you can let the seeds germinate in the warm and plant the baby seedlings outside in late spring, when the nights are warmer. These are snap bean seeds.

If your beans start to grow in all directions, You can bend them around the canes

3 YOUR BEANS WILL GROW UP THE CANES EASILY and may produce beautiful flowers, like those in the picture of the scarlet runners above. As they grow taller, you will need to tie the stems of your bean plants gently onto the canes.

4 WHEN YOUR BEANS ARE READY TO HARVEST, pick them frequently and they will keep producing more pods. You should pick pods from each plant every few days to prevent your beans from growing too big and too tough. Wash them and steam them so that you keep their fresh flavor.

Grow a monster pumpkin

Challenge your friends to a pumpkin-growing competition. One of the biggest so far is 1,800lb.—do you think you can beat that? Or, if you want to eat rather than compete, why not grow tasty winter squash to roast in the fall and winter.

You will need pots, potting mix, manure, pumpkin seeds

1 PLANT YOUR PUMPKIN SEEDS in pots and keep the seedlings well watered until they are ready to be planted outside. They are hungry and thirsty plants so when you do this you will need to dig a big hole, about 12in. deep and wide and fill the bottom with well-rotted manure to give them extra nutrients.

the science

REMOVING SIDESHOOTS
When a pumpkin plant grows it sends out a couple of strong-growing stems and puts all its pumpkin-producing energy into them. After a while, smaller sideshoots will start to appear and they will also try to produce pumpkins. To make sure that the main stems have lots of energy, you should take off these sideshoots so that your plant will produce one or two really big fruits.

Pumpkins love water so make sure you add plenty!

2 USE A PROTECTIVE COVER OVER YOUR SEEDLINGS. (You could use an upturned cut-in-half large plastic soda bottle.) Keep the seedlings well watered and feed them every week (or every few days if you want to grow a monster) with a liquid fertilizer.

3 IF YOU ARE TRYING TO GROW ONE REALLY BIG PUMPKIN, choose a single fruit that has developed early (it will have the longest possible time to grow) and take away all the other young fruits from the plant, putting them on your compost pile.

4 PICK PUMPKINS AND WINTER SQUASH in the fall in dry weather and before it gets too cold outside. They need a few days for their skins to "cure" in the sun if you want them to store well. Leave them somewhere dry, ideally not on the ground. If it looks like it might rain, bring your pumpkins inside and keep them dry.

Cut your pumpkin open, scoop out the seeds, wash them, and roast them for a tasty snack.

How to grow the best corn

Grow corn plants in a block, either in a circle or two rows, to make a forest of plants that will grow from small seedlings to leafy plants nearly 6½ft. high over the course of the summer.

Sow corn seeds in late spring. Young plants can be planted in midspring

When your corn plants are small, wrap them up in temporary row cover to protect them from the cold

1 CORN CANNOT BE PLANTED OUTSIDE until you are sure that the cold weather has passed, and they hate to sit in pots for too long, so don't sow them too early. Sow one seed per pot, indoors or in a hoop house.

the science

WIND POLLINATION

Many plants need to be pollinated before they can grow fruit. This means that pollen from the male flower has to make contact with the female flower. With some plants the pollen is carried by insects (particularly bees) or birds. Sometimes the wind carries the pollen into the air and hopefully onto the right part of the female flower. Corn is wind pollinated, so if the plants are close together there is more chance of pollen landing in the right place and producing good, full cobs of sweet corn.

2 YOUR CORN PLANTS will end up being really tall and, as you can see in the picture, once they have grown to the size of a ruler, they are strong and fast growing. Make sure you leave enough room between each plant for the leaves to spread out.

yum!

Corn on the BBQ Put a corn cob on a square of aluminum foil, spread the top of the cob with butter, and sprinkle on some salt and pepper. Wrap the foil up and then ask an adult to cook it on the barbecue for you. It will need to be cooked for around 30 minutes and will need to be turned over every few minutes.

Corn on the cob Fill a big saucepan with enough water to cover your corn cob, add a teaspoon of sugar, and ask an adult to help you to boil the water and add the cobs. They will be cooked when the kernels turn a darker color of yellow. Take them carefully out of the water and cover them in lots of butter, add salt and pepper, and then eat them messily ... but watch out, they will be very hot!

3 TO WORK OUT WHEN TO PICK YOUR CORN, watch out for when the end tassles begin to turn brown. If you think they might be ready, poke a fingernail into one of the yellow kernels; if a milky juice oozes out, the cob is ready to pick.

A stinky garlic garden

Lots of dishes, like pasta sauces, taste so much more exciting if you add garlic, and even better when you eat garlic bread with it too. And garlic is also really easy to grow!

You will need bulbs of garlic, grit for drainage, a hoe

Cover your gravel gently with a layer of soil. Use a hoe or a small fork to do this

1 FIRST USE TWINE to mark a straight line in your garden dirt. Garlic needs well-drained soil, so dig a shallow trench and sprinkle in some grit.

2 PILE UP THE SOIL OVER THE GRIT making a mound like a mountain. Pat it down gently with your hands.

Plant garlic cloves in early spring and harvest in the summer

3 BREAK YOUR GARLIC BULBS UP just before planting. You can use garlic you have bought in the supermarket but it is always better to buy garlic from a garden center as this will be free from diseases. Push the individual garlic segments (cloves) into the ground 4in. apart, until the tip of each clove is just below the surface of the soil.

4 GREEN SHOOTS AND TALL LEAVES TELL YOU that your garlic is growing. You will be able to pick your garlic the summer after you planted it, as soon as these leaves start to turn yellow. Use a fork to dig down under the bulbs and lift them up. Hang the garlic bulbs in an airy place to dry out before storing them, or use them fresh for a milder taste.

Yum!

To make garlic bread, peel a few cloves of garlic, crush them with the back of a spoon, and mix with soft butter and chopped parsley. Cut a baguette into slices, but don't cut all the way through into the bottom crust. Add garlic butter to the slices. Wrap the loaf in aluminum foil and ask an adult to bake it for about 10 minutes, until the butter has melted. If you don't have much time, you can rub the top of buttered toast with peeled garlic for really quick garlic bread, like in the picture.

65

A strawberry fountain

Delicious, sweet strawberries grow well in pots. Fit lots of plants into a small space by stacking pots on top of each other, creating a tasty tower of berries.

Try out how many plants you need to fill your fountain before you start planting

1 CHOOSE A REALLY BIG POT AND A MEDIUM-SIZED POT. You are making a tower, with the smaller pot on top of the larger one. First fill the big pot about three-fourths full with potting mix, then put the smaller one inside it and fill around it to the top. Then fill the smaller pot. Make sure that the smaller pot doesn't feel wobbly, and use your hands to firm down the potting mix in both pots.

2 BEFORE YOU PLANT THEM, WATER YOUR PLANTS WELL. When they have had a good soaking, you can start planting them in your tower. Put your plants well apart, and cover the tower completely. Water all the plants well.

Yum!

Meringue mess Break up some meringue into lumps and mix these with lots of whipped cream and some freshly sliced strawberries. Messy like its name, but delicious. And if you want to try something different, add some raspberries too.

Strawberry sandwiches This might sound funny, but freshly picked strawberries make really delicious sandwiches. Slice them thinly (ask an adult to help) and add a thick layer of berry slices to fresh white bread, thickly spread with sweet butter. Sprinkle the fruit with crunchy sugar, add the other slice of bread, and eat them as quickly as you can as they won't keep. If you feel like treating yourself, you could add a layer of whipped cream before adding the second slice of bread and if you feel adventurous try adding a sprinkling of black pepper instead of the sugar. It really is good.

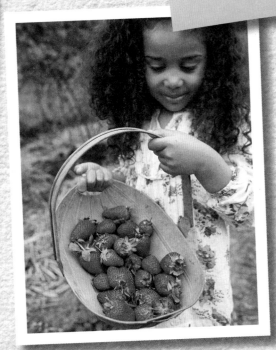

Plant your strawberries in the fall or early spring

3 FEED YOUR PLANTS EVERY TWO WEEKS with a high-potassium fertilizer such as liquid comfrey or liquid 5–5–10. This will help both flowers and then fruits to grow.

4 IN SUPERMARKETS, STRAWBERRIES OFTEN LOOK BEAUTIFUL but can be fairly tasteless. This may be because they have to be picked early, so they don't turn overripe and mushy on the journey from the farm to the store. You should leave yours on the plants until they are deep red before you eat them.

Grow your own fruit salad

Choose a corner of your garden for fruit. You will probably have to stop the birds from eating your fruit as it grows, which is most easily done by spreading special nets over your plants.

Raspberries

Raspberries are very strong-growing plants so you will need to stop them from taking over your garden. Dig a trench as a barrier between your raspberries and the rest of the garden or they will also appear in the middle of your garden where you don't want them.

Some raspberry plants can grow very large so it is a good idea to give these extra support. The best kind of raspberries to plant are fall raspberries as these need no support and you just have to cut the plants down to their base each winter to keep them strong.

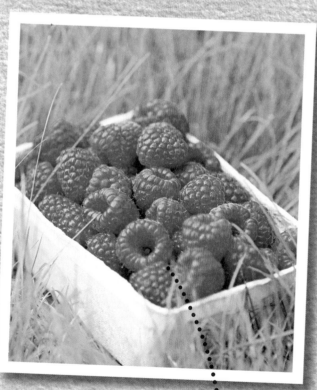

Raspberries are easy to grow and are fabulous with ice cream

Rhubarb

Rhubarb is really a vegetable, but gardeners treat it like a fruit so it deserves a place in your fruit garden. After planting rhubarb, water it while it gets settled in and then you will have to be patient. It takes two years for rhubarb stems to be ready to harvest. But NEVER eat the flowers because they are poisonous.

Blueberries

Blueberries like acidic soil. If your soil is not acidic, or you are not sure, it is best to grow them in pots of acidic-soil mix, which is perfect for them. Water the bushes with rainwater, if possible. Blueberries grow on neat little bushes and have beautiful glowing red leaves in the fall. Pick the fruits as soon as they ripen.

Plant fruit bushes in late fall or early spring, and rhubarb in spring

Blueberries are called "superfoods" because they are so good for you. Tasty too!

the science

ACIDIC-POTTING SOIL
Lots of plants like certain kinds of soil. Some plants, such as blueberries, are very fussy and like their soil to be acidic. But don't panic if you want to grow blueberries and don't have the right soil in your yard; you can buy special potting soil called acidic-soil mix from garden centers and use it to grow them.

Make a pizza herb garden

Pizza is simple to make—all you need is a base, a sauce, and some toppings. Sauces for pizza are at their tastiest when they include fresh homegrown tomatoes and lots of herbs like oregano, basil, and parsley. Make a pizza-shaped herb garden and fill each slice with a different herb. Add other tasty herbs like sage and rosemary and, when they have grown, you can get cooking and eating.

You will need a stick and some garden twine, some stones or gravel to mark your circle, and plants

1 YOU CAN USE TWINE TIED TO TWO STICKS to mark out a circle. Push one stick into the ground where you want the middle of your circle to be and then draw the circle with the other. Use more twine to divide your herb garden into sections, like slices of pizza.

2 PLANT PARSLEY, OREGANO, GARLIC, SAGE, dwarf prostrate (growing low to the ground) rosemary, chives, arugula, and fennel. Or you could just choose your favorites and plant up alternate "slices," maybe using colored gravel in between to separate them.

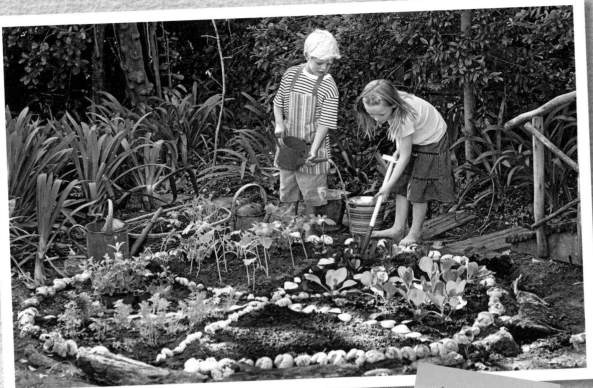

3 PICK HERBS AS YOU NEED THEM, but do try to do this regularly (or trim them) as it helps to keep the plants in good shape. Each time you remove the tender tips, you encourage sideshoots to form lower down the plant, keeping it bushy.

Sow oregano and parsley in early spring or early fall and basil all through spring

Yum!

To make a tasty pizza sauce using your herbs, start off by gently frying a chopped onion until it is soft and shiny, adding some chopped garlic toward the end. Pour on a carton of chopped tomatoes and let this bubble away for a few minutes until it thickens up. A pizza sauce shouldn't be watery. You can buy pizza bases or make your own. Spread your base with your sauce and then add your favorite pizza toppings together with loads of your homegrown herbs.

71

Giant smiley sunflowers

You can plant enormous sunflowers in your veg garden. Sunny and happy-looking, these plants also have masses of seeds that will attract birds to your garden.

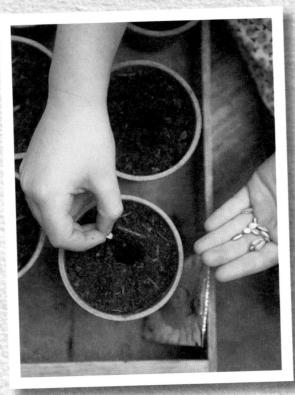

Sow these huge seeds indoors in midspring, or directly in the ground outside in late spring

1 SUNFLOWER SEEDS ARE QUITE BIG AND SO ARE THEIR SEEDLINGS, so you need to sow only one seed in each pot. Harden the little plants off carefully, taking the pots outside for short times when the weather is good, and plant your seedlings outside only when the weather is warmer.

2 SUNFLOWERS GROW REALLY TALL and their flowerheads can be huge, so they will probably need some extra support. Push a stake into the ground next to the stem and tie the plant's stem loosely to it. Feed frequently with a liquid fertilizer to help it to grow.

3 YOU CAN MAKE A PATTERN, A SMILE, OR EVEN WRITE YOUR NAME IN THE FLOWER'S FACE by pulling out florets (the collections of little flowers that make up the single big flowerhead). As the flower grows, your picture will still be there.

sunflowers have seeds that birds love to eat

4 WHEN THE PETALS START TO FALL OFF YOUR SUNFLOWER, SCRAPE THE SEEDS FROM ITS "FACE." You can use these to treat the birds—hang the entire flowerhead from the branches of a tree and they will love this nutritious winter food.

the science

STAKING AND TYING

When we grow tall plants like sunflowers in pots or in our yards, they may need some extra support to keep them standing up straight. Tomatoes, which often grow really tall but don't have strong woody stems, really like help to keep them upright—especially when they are young. You can use special bamboo canes, but broom handles or long sticks will work just as well. Make sure you tie the stems carefully, so that you do not damage the plants themselves.

73

Keeping your crops tip-top

Fruit and vegetables often ripen all at once or so quickly that you can get tired of eating them every day. Store them properly or freeze them and you can enjoy them at another time.

Potatoes

When you harvest your long-season potatoes, leave them in the sun for a few hours. Eat up any that are damaged or have holes in them where slugs could be hiding. Then brush off the soil and pack them into burlap bags. Take them all out once a month and check for soft or rotten ones, which you should throw away immediately.

Apples

Apples store best in wooden slatted boxes. They should be kept somewhere cool but away from frost and they need plenty of air. A basement is a good place, although you may have to throw some burlap or old bedding over them in really cold weather. Only store perfect apples and check them often. Throw away any that have gone moldy.

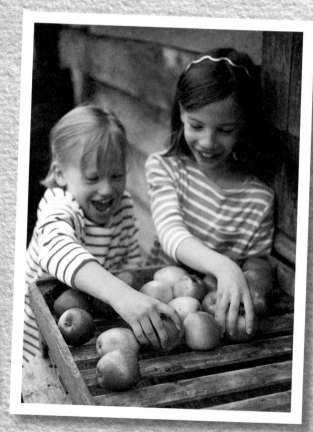

Berries

Raspberries and blackberries can easily be frozen. Spread them out on a cookie sheet and put this into the freezer so that each berry freezes individually. When they have been frozen, you can then put them into bags or boxes. Doing it this way takes a little longer, but it prevents the berries from sticking together in a big lump and means you can take as many or as few as you need.

Make your own popsicles

Making popsicles is a great way of using up fruit, and you can store them for ages—but you will probably want to eat them quickly and make more. First mash your fruit to make it a thick liquid called a purée. Apples will need to be cooked with a little sugar to do this, but strawberries, raspberries, and plums can just be whizzed up in a food processor with a little water or fruit juice. Pour the purée into popsicle molds and freeze.

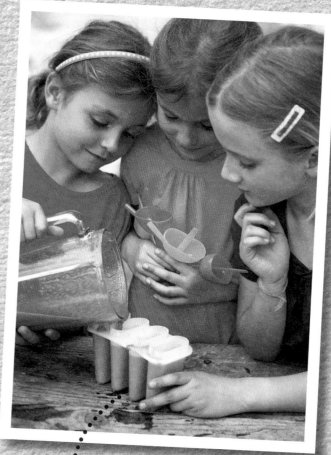

Mash up strawberries and freeze them to make smoothie lollies to share with your friends

How to make free pots for your plants

Start making paper pots in winter, ahead of seed—sowing time, so you will be ready when the busy season comes

You don't have to buy lots of pots for sowing seeds—you can make them out of old newspapers. And as well as being free, they rot away when planted in the ground, so they are also good for the planet.

You will need lots of old newspaper, a rolling pin, and a mug it fits into snugly—or, like in the photos, a pot-making kit

1 BEFORE YOU CAN START, CUT A PILE OF STRIPS OF NEWSPAPER about 10in. long and 3½in. wide. You don't need the pot maker shown above—you can use a wooden rolling pin and a mug into which it fits snugly.

2 ROLL THE PIECES OF NEWSPAPER AROUND THE ROLLING PIN OR POT MAKER, leaving a border of paper at the bottom. Tuck this up inside the newspaper tube.

Carefully fold in the bottom of the newspaper

3 AFTER YOU HAVE TUCKED IN THE NEWSPAPER BORDER put the paper tube into the cup and slide out the rolling pin. Make sure the newspaper covers the bottom of your pot. (Before doing this, you can use sticky tape to fasten the walls of your pot, but make sure you take it off before you plant them in the soil.)

4 FILL YOUR POTS WITH SOIL and stack them next to each other in a seed flat or shallow cardboard box. This will help them to stay upright. Sow large seeds such as beans directly into them, or use them when replanting ("pricking on") seedlings.

5 WHEN THE SEEDLINGS ARE BIG ENOUGH TO PLANT OUTDOORS, plant the pots straight into the ground. The roots will quickly push through the soft, wet newspaper, and the newspaper will gradually rot away. Magic ... and totally free!

Peas: treats you can eat direct from the plants

Peas really do taste best if you grow your own. This is because the sugar they contain starts to change to starch as soon as they are picked, so eating them straight from the plant is always going to be the best. You can eat them sneakily while you are gardening, fresh in salads, or when they have been cooked very quickly in boiling water.

Watch out!

Rabbits, birds, and mice love pea seeds and, if they get the chance, they will start nibbling them as soon as you've sown them. Keep your seeds safe by sowing them into a length of plastic roof guttering filled with potting mix. You can hang this out of the reach of rabbits and mice until the seeds have germinated ("sprouted").

1 PLANT OUT YOUR PEA SEEDLINGS when they are a few inches tall. If you have been growing them in roof guttering, dig out "gutter-shaped" trenches in your soil and slide in groups of the seedlings, together with the potting mix. If you haven't used guttering, just plant them direct into the soil.

Sow pea seeds in the middle of either spring or fall

2 PEA PLANTS LOVE TO CLIMB, so give them a climbing frame to scramble up. A row of sticks or twiggy prunings pushed firmly into the soil is perfect.

3 PEAS CAN BE TRAINED to grow up a tepee of canes, placed either in soil or over a pot. Keep gently pushing their stems into the support and they will climb up.

4 THE MORE YOU PICK YOUR PEAS, the more pods your plants will produce. So keep eating the peas as soon as they are ready to pick—you can be a real pea pig!

Pop delicious sweet little peas into your mouth direct from the plant

Six weeks until the big crunch

Growing carrots is super speedy. You can grow them in the ground, but they also grow really well in deep containers or raised beds, where they enjoy the loose, easily drained soil.

Always read the seed packet instructions carefully

Watch out!

Carrot rust flies smell carrots when they fly low over the ground. But you can be cleverer than them—if you grow carrots in a pot, you can keep the pots above the level at which carrot rust flies fly. Don't worry, they won't realize that they should make a detour. If your carrots are in the ground, put up a 2ft. "fence" of plastic sheeting along the row and the flies won't be able to get to your carrots! You can also cover up the carroty smell by growing garlic, onions, and herbs along your carrot row. Carrot rust flies also attack parsnips, parsley, and celery.

1 TO PLANT CARROTS directly into the ground, make a long, shallow hole (called a seed drill) and sow your seeds along it. If you are growing your carrots in pots, scatter your seeds over the top and then sprinkle a light covering of potting mix over the top. Water the seeds and, if you are sowing them early in the year, cover the seeds with temporary row cover to keep them warm and help them to germinate (sprout).

Sow in midspring or summer. Any you sow in summer will be ready to store for roasting in winter—yum!

YUM!

Little carrots are really sweet and are the perfect size to dip. Blend some cream cheese, sour cream, garlic, and some of your herbs, and use your baby carrots to eat it all up. Try using pieces of cucumber or little florets of broccoli and cauliflower too.

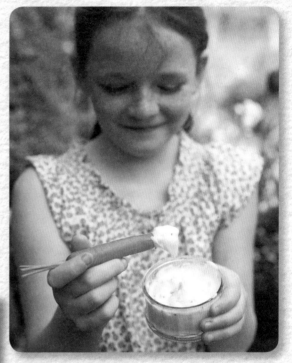

2 WHEN YOUR PLANTS START TO GROW, start taking out a few plants from the row to make extra room (thinning out). You can wash and eat the young carrots, if you like.

3 YOUNG RAW CARROTS ARE WONDERFULLY SWEET and crunchy, but any you leave in the ground will just keep on growing until you are ready to pull them up and cook them. It's a good idea to sow some carrots in the summer just so that you will have carrots to pick later in the season for storing into winter.

Carrots are ready for munching just six weeks after sowing—but big carrots like these will take longer!

Be a green gardener

Insect wildflower heaven

Because they are rich in nectar—a sugary liquid that bees and butterflies love—growing wildflowers is the best way to encourage insects to visit your yard. You don't need much room for a wildflower garden and lots of insects will visit and spread pollen from plant to plant.

1 BEFORE YOU BEGIN, MAKE SURE YOU GET RID of as many weeds as possible and use a rake to break up any big lumps of soil on the surface.

Getting ready

Your wildflower garden won't be exactly the same as anything you see in rural areas, but you can use your own mixture of flower seeds to create a garden that looks very much like a prairie. Try sowing some of these seeds, and you will like the results almost as much as the insects do:

Field poppy • cornflower • California poppy • corn marigold • black-eyed Susan • larkspur • love-in-a-mist • ox-eye daisy

2 SOW HANDFULS OF YOUR SEED MIXTURE in a zigzag. Then it will cover a large area and look natural.

Mix your choice of seeds together in a pot before sowing them in the ground

84

3 ONCE YOU HAVE SCATTERED YOUR SEEDS, use a rake to make sure they are lightly covered in soil. Water the site well using a water breaker.

4 WHY NOT MAKE A SEED BALL so that you can sow wildflower seeds in unloved areas? To do this, you will need to mix flower seeds and potting mix in a bucket with three times as much powdered clay. Add water until it is squelchy enough to squeeze the mixture into balls the size of a golf ball. Leave these to dry and then, ideally in the early fall, throw them into your chosen patch of bare land. The fall rain will soften your seed balls and, with luck, flowers will grow in the spring.

A wildflower area is really beautiful, and insects will find it just as lovely as you will

Exploring a watery wildlife paradise

You don't need a pond to add water to your garden. You can bury an old bucket or dishwashing bowl in the ground and fill it with water. Don't forget that adding water to your garden may bring frogs and toads and these will also eat slugs, the No. 1 garden enemy!

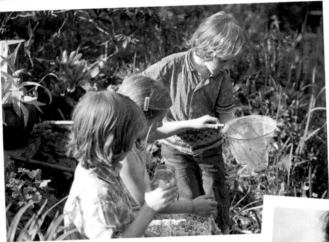

Pond dipping

If you do have a pond, take some water out of it with a bucket. Then wave a fishing net in the pond. If you find any minibeasts in the net, empty them into the bucket for a closer look. Or you may find some wobbly frogspawn jelly.

Fantastic frogspawn

Don't worry, if you don't have your own pond, you can still hatch tadpoles. In the spring collect a jar of frogspawn from a local pond and put it in a bucket or fishbowl. It is probably too hard without a pond to look after the frogspawn all the way from blobs of jelly to frogs, so hatch them and then return them to the pond where you collected them.

Planting for ponds

Plants are really important to ponds. They make shady spaces on the pond edges—these give shelter to wildlife and help to keep the pond water cool. Some plants even grow under the water and add oxygen to the water, which is good for pond animals.

Help wildlife to thrive

A wildlife pond needs sloping edges so that animals can crawl in and out easily. Other animals can use the edges to stand and drink fresh water from the pond without falling in. A gravel slope is perfect.

87

Home, sweet home for your birds

Birds can sometimes be a nuisance in your yard by eating berries. But they also eat pests so you should welcome them into your garden—just be careful to protect any fruit ripening in your plot.

Birds need water too

Birds need water year-round. Put a birdbath somewhere where there are no cats nearby. But make sure it is also fairly close to a bush or tree where birds can escape to if they sense danger. Keep the birdbath topped up, especially on hot summer days or in the winter, when it's really cold and you may need to break the ice.

the science

THE IMPORTANCE OF BIRDS

Birds are really important in the yard because they kill pests like slugs and other creatures that will want to eat your vegetables. There are lots of ways to get birds to visit your garden but making sure there is water is a very good way to bring them in. Birds are very clean creatures and need to look after their feathers, so you can enjoy watching them wash in the birdbath.

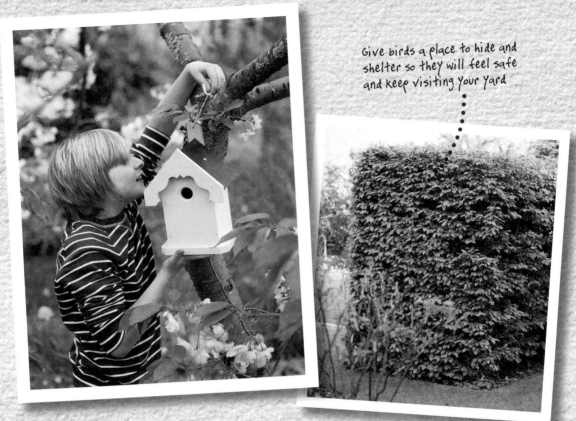

Give birds a place to hide and shelter so they will feel safe and keep visiting your yard

Lots of shelter

Birds need lots of different places to shelter around the yard. They particularly love thick hedges, which serve as a place where they can live safe from predators. Hedges are also a "wildlife corridor," making bridges from one wildlife-friendly place to another. If you have plenty of space and trees, hang some birdhouses in trees and bushes—birds can shelter there during the day and they may return in the spring to nest in them.

Keeping crops safe from birds

Growing fruit in a fruit cage (a huge frame covered with a net) is the best way to keep birds away. If you can't do this, keep some netting ready to cover fruits like cherries and raspberries as they start to ripen. Make sure that you stretch the net as tightly as possible and secure it firmly—if the net flaps about, birds can get caught in it. Take the net away each time you pick your fruit and then take it off completely when the whole crop has been picked—then the birds can come in and eat any pests left behind.

Great homes for birds

Put up a birdhouse in your yard because, if you are lucky, baby birds will be born there. It's more difficult to do this if you live in an apartment so why not share a birdhouse with a friend who has a yard?

What birdhouse should I choose?

If you live in an urban area, choose a small birdhouse because birds such as sparrows like them better than a larger one. If you live in a rural area, put up a larger birdhouse for woodpeckers or thrushes. A birdhouse with an open front is perfect for robins.

What should it be made of?

Wood is great for birdhouses, as is "woodcrete," which is a mixture of wood and concrete. Try to make sure that the wood is long-lasting hardwood. Birdhouses should have holes in the base to let things drain away and holes in the top to let in the air.

Why not ask for a birdhouse for your next birthday?

Decorate a birdhouse with your favorite colors and stickers

Where should I put my birdhouse?

Ask an adult to help you to fix your birdhouse on a tree, wall, or post 6–12ft. above the ground. Choose a site where the entrance is sheltered from wind, rain, and strong sunlight. Tilt the birdhouse forward a little so that rain won't fall into the entrance. Make sure birds can fly easily to and from your birdhouse. Open-fronted birdhouses should be secured about 6ft. from the ground and their entrances should be hidden by trees, bushes, or branches.

How do I look after it?

Birds will be less likely to come back to your birdhouse if it is filled with last year's twigs and leaves. You should clear out all this garbage between late summer and midwinter. Before you do this, watch the birdhouse for a few days to be sure no birds are using it, then open it up. Trash any garbage. Wash the birdhouse out with hot water (but don't use soap or dish-washing detergent) and leave it to dry.

I wonder which birdhouse the birds will like best?

91

A bird-feeder buffet

Mixing bird seed with suet or lard will give the birds extra nutrients that they can store for the cold winter months. It also binds the seeds so they can be made into cakes to hang up.

You will need half a coconut shell, suet/lard, wild bird-seed mix, twine

1 ASK AN ADULT TO HELP YOU TO MELT A BLOCK OF SUET (a kind of fat) in a saucepan and then add just enough wild bird food to give every seed a generous coating of suet. Give it a good stir because dry bits will not stick together. If you can't find suet in your shop, you can use lard instead.

2 ASK AN ADULT TO MAKE A HOLE IN THE bottom half of a coconut shell or an old yogurt pot. (Do NOT try to cut the coconut yourself as it is VERY hard.) Thread some twine with a knot tied in one end through the hole.

3 SPOON THE FATTY SEEDY MIXTURE IN, pressing it down firmly. It won't look tasty to you but the birds will love it. Leave to set.

4 ONCE THE FATTY MIXTURE HAS SET, hang your coconut or yogurt pot from a high spot, like the branch of a tree. It should be too difficult for cats to reach. Choose a shady spot, as the fat will melt if it gets too warm. You could also hang seed feeders of peanuts and rings of apple for the birds. You will now be able to watch birds visit, knowing that they are filling themselves up with fats to help them through the cold winter nights.

Don't forget to keep your seed feeders topped up with wild bird-seed mix too—birds need lots of help

93

Bees need homes too

Bees, like lots of insects, are very good friends to gardeners. In the winter, they like to crawl into small spaces to keep safe and warm. You can make them the perfect winter home using bits and pieces.

1 ASK AN ADULT TO CUT A BUNCH OF HOLLOW-STEMMED BAMBOO CANES to about the same length as a ruler. Using garden twine, tie them together tightly at each end.

2 MAKE A HANDLE for your insect house by tying another piece of twine between the other twine, leaving a long loop so you can hang it from the branch of a tree.

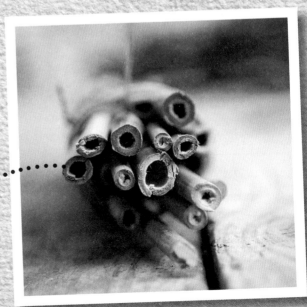

Bees like to nest in small spaces, but all sorts of other insects will visit your insect house as long as it has spaces of different sizes

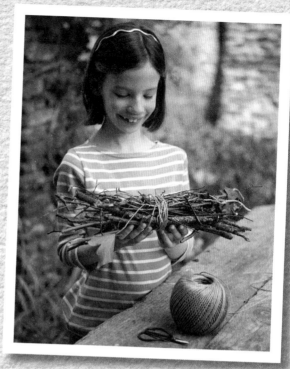

3 MAKE A WILDLIFE HOTEL AS WELL. Find an old bookcase or ask an adult to make some shelves out of pieces of plywood, and then put dividers in to make a series of small boxes. Fill these with stick bundles, bricks with holes in them, old pieces of wood, bundles of straw and twigs, and whatever else you find that you think might make a good refuge for an insect.

4 IF YOU DON'T HAVE ANY BAMBOO YOU CAN USE TWIGS to make your insect house or hotel. Tie twigs of the same length together and find a dry, cosy place to push them into—perhaps into or under a hedge, or along the side of a shed. The insects will soon move in.

Going batty

Gardens with lots of insects are often visited by bats and it's very exciting to see them swooping around on summer evenings. To encourage them into your yard, try to plant lots of flowers that smell good. These will attract the insects that bats eat. You should also make plenty of winter homes for insects as then there will always be food for any bats that are visiting. You could also build a bat box, which is a bit like a birdhouse but doesn't have a bottom. A pond or some other water nearby will also help bats to make a home in your yard. You could just sink an old bucket into the ground and fill it with water—but be careful that it is somewhere safe where nobody can fall into it or step into it by mistake.

Worms can make plant food

You can use bits of leftover food from your kitchen to make compost and liquid fertilizer. If you add a handful of "tiger" worms to your wormery, they will eat up your scraps and, in return, they will even turn them into compost and liquid fertilizer for you.

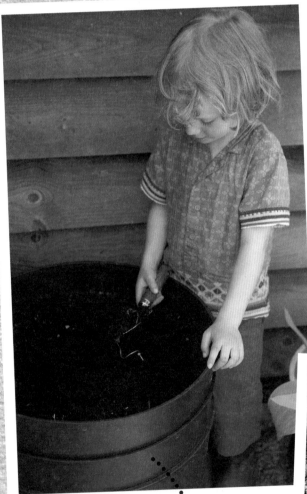

Wormeries are great fun. There are two sorts. Some have a series of trays through which the worms move as they eat the waste and make compost in return. It is easy to take the compost out of this sort of wormery—you just wait until all the worms have moved into the next tray, then lift it out. Others are more like a large bin from which you can take free compost every six months or so.

Your wriggly worms

When you buy a wormery, it comes with a pack of special worms. Put them in the wormery with some shredded newspaper for their bedding and a handful of veg scraps from the kitchen, chopped up small.

The wriggly worms move from layer to layer, leaving great things behind

It takes the worms a while to settle into their new home, but once they start eating at full speed you should be able to put most of the scraps from your kitchen into your wormery. Every now and again, you will need to sprinkle the worm compost with some calcified seaweed, which probably came with your wormery. Adding this will keep the compost just as the worms like it. You can also add crushed eggshells.

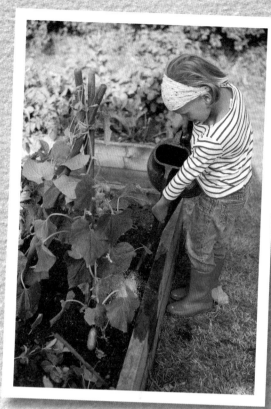

Using your wormery juice

Use the wormery's special tap to take away the liquid fertilizer the worms make, or else the compost the worms also make may be too wet. Add water to this liquid to make a fantastic free fertilizer for all your plants.

They don't just sting you

Another way of producing your own fertilizer is to crush some nettle or comfrey plants (wear strong gloves while you're doing this) and leave them to soak in a bucket of water for three or four weeks. The bucket will get very smelly, so put it well away from the house. When it has soaked thoroughly, mix a small amount of the smelly liquid with 10 times as much water as you have smelly liquid. Pour this into a mister, and on a still day spray this mixture (which will be really rich in nitrogen) onto the leaves of your plants.

New plants for nothing

You don't have to buy new plants—just learn how to grow new ones from the ones you have already. Taking cuttings, collecting seeds, and dividing up your plants are easy ways to grow more ... for free!

Make new plants in the fall and spring by splitting plants into more than one or by growing new ones from cuttings

Collecting seeds

You can gather seeds easily from snap, scarlet runner, and fava beans, peas, chili peppers, and lettuce. To grow seeds to plant for next year's crops, first you will need to choose the plant from which you are going to collect seed. Then don't pick anything from that plant as it grows. When the plant's crop is finished, choose a dry day to harvest your seeds. Pick off the seed pods, pop them open, pick out the seeds, and store them in a dry airtight container away from the sun. Then you will be able to grow new plants next season for nothing!

Store collected seeds in an airtight container in a cool, dark spot, and sow them the following year

the science

GROWING NEW PLANTS FROM CUTTINGS

Seeds can remain dormant (not starting to grow) until they are happy with the conditions around them. In spring, when the days start to get longer and warmer, it's a good time for them to grow. This also makes spring a good time to take cuttings. Plants contain a group of cells known as the cambium, which helps them to grow roots. As the plants start to grow in spring, the cambium cells begin to work and there is a greater chance that your cutting will produce roots.

making baby plants

If you want lots of herbs, take cuttings from the ones you already have. Grow sage, rosemary, thyme, and lemon verbena from cuttings in spring. Cut a stem about 4in. long, with no flowers on it. Take off any leaves from the bottom third of the stem and push it into a pot filled with potting mix, right up to the leaves. Water, cover the pot with a clear plastic bag, seal it, and put it on the windowsill. You will know the cutting has rooted when new leaves start to appear.

Before you buy new plants, learn how to grow more from the ones you own already

splitting up your plants

Some plants can be divided (split up) in the fall—herbs such as mint and thyme, for example. Ask an adult to help you to lift the whole plant from the ground and then, between you, use a spade and your weight to split it in half. If the plant is really big, you may want to split it up again, into four or even smaller pieces. Replant all the plants right away and give them lots of water.

Growing from "runners"

Strawberries grow "runners," which are long stems that root where they land and make new plants. It is easy to dig these up and put them in pots. You can give these away to friends but you will need to start again from new plants every three years.

Oh no!
What has
happened?

What's gone wrong?

Here are a few of the problems that you can have with your crops.

But if you are ready for them, you won't have many disasters.

Slugs and snails

These little terrors cause the most problems in vegetable gardens. They can eat a whole row of seedlings in one night and can cause huge amounts of damage to young plants. You need to turn to page 106 for ideas on how to deal with them because you really can't let them beat you!

Snails might be fun to watch as they slither along, but they will eat your young plants

Sap suckers

Aphids are pests that swarm over the soft parts of plants and suck out their sap (the liquid that moves food and water around your plants). They stop plants from growing well and the plant may become sticky. Look on page 104 for ways to encourage aphid-eating insects to eat your pests.

Wiggly caterpillars

Caterpillars nibble holes in leaves. On most plants this isn't a big problem, but some caterpillars can take all the leaves from a plant very fast and so weaken it. Some plants such as cabbages are particular favorites of caterpillars.

Not enough water?

If you don't water your seedlings enough after you have planted them, they will look sad and floppy. Make sure you give them lots to drink every day until their roots have grown big enough to find water in the soil themselves.

Your vegetables will be small and less tasty if you do not remember to water them regularly

Danger from the skies

Birds can pull up onions, shred, and eat brassicas (another name for members of the cabbage family), eat ripe berries, and even seeds before they have germinated. Put nets over your fruit bushes and cabbages as soon as you plant them outside. Try making a scarecrow to keep birds away from your seeds. You will find more ideas on page 108.

Your plants' best friends

Some plants get along with each other better than others. "Companion planting" is when one plant really helps the one that it is planted next to. Perhaps the smell of one hides the smell of the other and keeps pests away, or maybe one plant attracts pests and keeps them off the one you are growing to eat. By helping each other, these plants are "good companions." Here are some ideas.

Beans and nasturtiums—aphids like eating beans, but they love nasturtiums even more. The nasturtiums act as "trap" or "decoy" plants, luring the aphids away from your crop.

Carrots and onions—carrot rust flies find their favorite food (carrots!) by smelling them, but the smell of onions confuses the flies and makes it harder for them to find the carrots.

Cabbages and dill—hoverflies and other insects that eat aphids really like dill so, with dill on offer, they will leave your cabbages alone. Dill is also a great herb to eat, especially with fish.

Tomatoes and French marigolds—aphids are said to hate the smell of French marigolds so they keep away.

Fruit trees and poached-egg plants—poached-egg plants attract lots of good insects, some of which will find their way onto your fruit trees and spread pollen between them, encouraging fruit.

Ladybeetles can protect your plants by munching on aphids and other garden insects

Corn, beans, and winter squash—the squash shades the roots of the other plants, while the corn provides a "pole" for the beans to grow up.

Tomatoes and basil—growing basil with tomatoes may make them taste better.

Basil and tomatoes taste delicious together, so why not grow them together too?

"Good companions" are plants that help each other

Aphids think that the smell of French marigolds is horrible, so if you grow them near tomatoes the aphids will stay away from both plants.

Smelly onions will confuse carrot rust flies and stop them from finding and destroying your carrot crop

The great vegetable destroyers

Your vegetables' main enemies are slugs and snails. But don't panic, there are lots of weapons you can use against them.

Slugs and snails love young, soft plants and can eat a whole row of seedlings or baby plants overnight. Although you might see them during the day, they are at their most dangerous at night, when it is cooler and damper and they find it easier to move around and munch. Although barriers and slug hotels work, slug pellets are the best way to keep slugs away. But they can be poisonous so choose pellets that contain a chemical called aluminum sulfate as these are the least likely to harm other animals. Be very careful with slug pellets as they can poison you too so always ask an adult to help you with them.

The slug hotel

Make a slug hotel (a trap for slugs) by burying a glass jar or plastic container in the ground just up to the top of the container. Fill it with beer and the slugs will come slithering in, following the smell of the beer. Once they have visited, they won't be allowed to leave as they will drown in the beer—so empty them away each morning.

the science

SLUG BARRIERS
If you turn a slug or snail upside down you'll find a large area called a foot underneath it. This foot is what enables these creatures to get around, but in order to work properly it needs a smooth, damp surface. Putting down barriers of something dry and rough like gravel makes it more difficult for the slug or snail to move. Make a ring of sharp grit around your plants—this will help keep slugs away.

Ask an adult to give you some beer for your slug hotel. Any type of beer will do

A line of gravel or grit will help keep the slugs and snails away—but make sure there are no gaps in your barrier (or the slugs will find them) and also add some slug pellets to your gravel. But be careful!

You can even crush up old eggshells and use these to make a sharp and pointy slug "wall." Like the gravel barrier, it's a good idea to mix in some slug pellets — but remember they can be poisonous to you too

107

(Not so) scary scarecrows!

Scarecrows are great fun to make but even the best ones don't seem to scare the birds away for long. Make your own scarecrow, using old clothes—choose a funny combination as your scarecrow can look as strange as you like.

1 FIND TWO PIECES OF LUMBER— one about half as long as the other—and ask an adult to nail them together to make a cross. Old broom handles work well. The shorter piece will become the arms of the scarecrow, and the longer one will go into the ground.

2 STUFF A PAIR OF OLD PANTS with straw or another stuffing material, like scrunched-up newspapers or other old clothes. Tie twine around the pant bottoms to hold in the stuffing. Put a shirt onto the "arms" of the cross and then ask an adult to roughly sew the pants to the bottom of the shirt, or you can use old suspenders to hang the pants from the scarecrow's arms. Stuff the shirt with straw and tie the cuffs together with twine so that the stuffing stays in the shirt, too.

3 NOW MAKE A HEAD. This can be an old soccer ball, a pumpkin, an upturned bucket, or anything round and light. You can even make your own head from an old pillowcase that you can stuff. Don't put its head on yet.

4 WHEN YOU HAVE FINISHED YOUR SCARECROW choose its spot in the yard and ask an adult to use a mallet to bang it deep into the ground. Now you can add your scarecrow's head to the top of the pole and even add an old hat or scarf if you have one.

A scarecrow may not keep birds away from your plants for long but it will look great anyway!

Other scary things!

While scarecrows look great and are a lot of fun to make, birds can get used to them and stop being scared by them. Scarers that make a noise or flash in the sunlight work much better and will keep birds away for longer, even though they will get used to these too.

Twirly pinwheels

Jazzy toy pinwheels are great for scaring birds away for short times. Tie them onto your fence or plant them in a flowerpot. Even when there's only a little bit of wind, they will spin around and their colors will flash in the sunshine, keeping the birds away.

Flashing lights

Hang lines of shiny beads in the sunshine and they will sparkle in the light as they move in the wind. Old CDs are also perfect for this and already have a hole in the middle which you can loop twine through.

Birds can get used to scarers really quickly. Use brightly colored pinwheels like these only for as long as you really need them—such as when your berries are ripening. Next time, try something else!

Noisy scarers

You can make a bell-chime scarer like this one with a piece of wood, twine, and old bells of various sizes. You can buy bells in craft stores or take them from old cat or dog collars. Cut a long bit of twine and tie it to each end of the wood. Cut some twine for each bell and tie onto the twig in a row. Make sure you leave just enough space between the bells so that they touch each other when the wind blows and make a jangling, tinkling sound.

If you don't like the sound of bells, collect shells, beads, and bits of wood, and tie some twine around each. If you need to make holes in anything, ask an adult to help you. Tie your collection of things to pieces of twine, and wrap them around an old coat hanger, making sure that the lines are close enough for the shells and beads to knock together

Index

Acknowledgments

All photographs are by Will Heap for Octopus Publishing, apart from the following:
Bigstock sdenness 40 right, 63 below
Fotolia awfoto 95 above left; benamalice 73 above; ChristopheB 100-1; Denis Nata 63 centre; Edyta Pawlowska 68; fdoimages 71 below; merryll 65 above right
GAP Photos Dave Bevan 105 below; David Dixon 54 below; Fiona Lea/design Sue Beesley 87 above; Friedrich Strauss 72 right; Graham Strong 105 above; Martin Hughes-Jones 62; Mel Watson 67 left; Paul Debois 18 left; Zara Napier 79 above right, 103 below
Getty Images D Normark/PhotoLink 63 above; Sudo Takeshi 98 below
Octopus Publishing Group Anton de Beer18 right, 70 left & right, 71 above, 90 above, 108-111; Freia Turland 19 left, 102 above & below
Thinkstock Comstock 32 above; Hemera 1, 5 below, 30 above, 36, 37 above & below, 75 above, 78 right, 88 above, 95 below, 96 right, 103 above; iStockphoto 8-9, 31 below, 37 centre, 38 left, 59 all, 60 above & below, 74 left, 78 left, 79 above left, below left & right, 90 below, 107 above; Jupiterimages 30 below, 42-3, 61 above & below; Martin Poole 49 above; Medioimages/Photodisc 41 right, 73 below

Daisy, windmill, notepaper and tag used throughout: Fotolia/ecco; Fotolia/barneyboogles; Thinkstock/iStockphoto; Thinkstock/Hemera

The publishers would like to thank the following:

Mary Caroe for allowing us to photograph in her beautiful gardens (www.vanngarden.co.uk); **Emily Caroe** for making us so welcome; **our models:** Isobel Brooks Anastasia and Joseph Glass; Carla, Ashleigh and Emily Rochester; Hugo Brown; Emily and Daniel Scartlebury; Mary, Calum and Penny Skuodas; Tom, Scarlet and Stanley Heap; Mia and Scarlett Somerville; Reece Merritt; **Boden** for loaning us the gorgeous clothes (www.bodenusa.com); **Crocus** for the loan of the fantastic garden tools and other wonderful things (www.crocus.co.uk.)

About the authors

Chris Collins is Britain's children's television gardener. His RHS Campaign for School Gardening gave over one million children in the UK access to school gardens. In 2007, he was awarded the Duke of Edinburgh medal for his services to horticulture.

Lia Leendertz writes about gardening for UK publications including *Gardens Illustrated*, *Gardens*, and the *Guardian Weekend* magazine. Her most recent book is *The Twilight Garden* and her blog *Midnight brambling* was chosen by the Garden Media Guild as blog of 2011.